kelly swanson
-STORY-LIBS

Kelly Swanson

Strategic Storytelling Expert

www.MotivationalSpeakerKellySwanson.com
1-800-303-1049

Kelly Swanson
Story Formula & Anatomy of a Presentation
Cheat Sheet

Story Formula:

Character + Conflict + Emotion + Resolution + Emotion + Victory Moment + Emotion + Lesson + Objection + Encouragement + Action Step

Anatomy of a Presentation:

Who Am I +
Why Am I Here +
What Do We Have In Common / Problem We Share +
What Happens If We Don't Fix It +
What Happens If We Do +
How Did I Experience This Problem +
What Perspective Shift Did I Have to Go Through +
What 3 Steps Helped Me Fix It +
I Know What You're Thinking +
Other Resources +
Action Steps +
Encouragement

Swanson Story-Libs™ : The *Elevator Pitch 1* Story-Lib

This story lib helps you tell people what you do in an emotionally compelling way
This Elevator Pitch Story-Lib is based on the **personal experience**.

My name is _____, but people call me _____, because
                 Your First Name   *Nickname*

_____. I am from
* Reason for Nickname

_____, which means _____.
City and State Where You Live/Were Born   ** Something Funny About Where You Are From*

Something most people wouldn't guess about me is that I

_____. I work for
* Share a quirk, weird habit or hobby – something that makes you human or interesting

_____ and my business card will tell you that I am a _____. But
Company Name   *Job Title/Role*

what I *really* do is help _____ people who are struggling with
                           What Kind of People

_____ and are feeling
Pains/Desires of the Ideal Person/People you want to impact with this story

_____. I can relate to this because
How They Feel Because of this Pain/Desire

_____ I was experiencing something very similar in my own life. I
How long ago – and what was going on at this time

was struggling to _____ and it was making me feel very
                State the struggle that is similar to theirs

3

_____. I thought the answer was
Tell us how you were feeling with emotions that would likely mirror theirs

_____. But it turns out, I
Wrong Ways You Tried to Fix Problem that Would be Similar to What Your Typical Client Is Doing

was wrong. That wasn't fixing the problem. I was focusing on _____ when I should have
                                                                Wrong Perspective

been focusing on _____. Once I figured that out, the rest just fell into place and my life and as
                  Right Perspective

a result, my life changed in these ways: _____. That's why I love what I
                                          State the difference in your life a a result

do and why I chose to _____ because we/they believe in
                       Start this company / Work for this company

_____. And we all know that when it comes to business, the people are
What your company is passionate about

what truly make the difference. The people we serve, and the people we serve beside. I like doing this

work because I get to help people _____ and it makes me
                                   Problems you help them fix or desires you help them reach

feel _____ to watch people _____ and this in
     Describe your emotions   *Describe the Specific Changes/Results in Their Lives*

turn helps them to _____. To me, this is
                    Describe the Difference In Their Lives in an even Bigger more Dramatic Way

more than a job. It's my calling. I guess you could even say it's my legacy. I think the world becomes a

better place when we all work together to

_____. I would love to hear more about your
Describe how your work affects the world and the generations to come

story. Would you like to meet for coffee?

4

*Reason For Nickname: If you don't have a nickname, here is a place to make up a funny one to get a cute laugh. For example, my name is Barbara, but my husband refers to me as his future ex-wife. (Perhaps you could Google funny terms of endearment for spouses and find one you like.)

* Something Funny About Where You are From: This is a good place to find more than one thing and get a few more laughs. Make fun of being from the South, or a big city, or a farm town. One quick way to get to some laughs is to say, "You know you're from a small town when…." Google it if you need to. If there is nothing interesting about the city you are from, talk about the state, or the neighborhood, or even what kind of family you were born into. You know you're a military kid when. Brainstorm a bunch of answers and pick a couple of your favorites or ones that happen to be funny or interesting.

* Share Something Interesting/Quirky that Most People Wouldn't Guess or is TOTALLY OBVIOUS about you: Were you a Dodge Ball champ in third grade? Were you the picked-on kid? Do you have any freaky phobias? Finding out someone's odd little quirks immediately endears them to us.

* Wrong Perspective: This is a great place to differentiate yourself from the competition by making it look like everybody else is looking at the wrong thing – but YOU have a different answer. An ENTIRELY new perspective that nobody has ever looked at before. And THIS will make all the difference. Like the guy in the movie City Slickers who kept holding up one finger and saying "It's all about that ONE thing." Convince your listener that you have the magic bullet. This story focuses on the bigger why instead of bombarding them in the elevator with all the hows. This is the teaser. Get them hooked on the why and they will hire you for the how to.

Swanson Story-Libs™ : The *Elevator Pitch 2* Story-Lib

This is the perfect story lib to help you tell people what you do in an emotionally compelling way.
This Elevator Pitch Story-Lib is based on the **customer testimonial**.

My name is _____, but people call me _____, because
 Your First Name *Nickname*

_____. I am from
* Reason for Nickname

_____, which means _____.
City and State Where You Live/Were Born ** Something Funny About Where You Are From*

Something most people wouldn't guess about me is that I

_____. I work for
* Share a quirk, weird habit or hobby – something that makes you human or interesting

_____ and my business card will tell you that I am a
Company Name

_____ which is really another name for _____. But
 Job Title/Role ** Something Funny About Your Job*

what I *really* do is help _____ people who are struggling with
 What Kind of People

_____ and are feeling
Pains/Desires of the Ideal Person/People you want to impact with this story

_____. I still remember when _____ came to me for help.
How They Feel Because of this Pain/Desire *Person/Couple's Name*

_____
Describe the person/couple with a few personal details so we get an image of them – details your ideal listener could rela

. They were really having a hard time. They were struggling with

6

_____ and it was making them feel
Problems They Were Having and What They Were Really Wishing For

_____ and as a result they were _____. They had tried
Emotions they were Having   *How Their Life was Painful as a Result*

everything and had gone to others for help and

_____ . I felt so bad for them. I knew
Results of Hiring The Wrong People and Spending Money In the Wrong Places

exactly what they were going through, because I had been through it myself when

_____. We sat down and I just
Explain in just a few sentences a time when you had a similar problem, and how you felt

listened to their story. Here at _____ we don't just _____, we
                         Company Name   *a boring way to describe what you do*

solve YOUR problems. And we know that each person has a unique story and a unique set of needs.

Once I was able to really understand their problem, research their options, and come up with a

solution based on years of working through similar situations, I realized where the problem was. They

had been trying to fix this problem for ten years, and in a month of using my _____ they
                                                                      Method/System/Process

were already seeing results. It was so exciting to watch. I saw _____ and over
                                                   Specific Outcomes in Their Life

time began to see even bigger things happen. _____.
                                                                            Describe the difference in their lives in a dramatic way

They've been customers for twenty years now. And like all of our customers, they really become our

family. That's why I love doing the work I do. It's for people like _____. I learned
                                                                              Name The Person/Couple again

early on in my career, that the work we do isn't just about the quality service we provide – but about the people we serve. With every story of another person we help, becomes another story in the scrapbook of our company. We have lots more stories on our website. Here's a link if you want to check it out. We'd love to hear your story. Want to meet for coffee?

***Reason For Nickname:** If you don't have a nickname, here is a place to make up a funny one to get a cute laugh. For example, my name is Barbara, but my husband refers to me as his future ex-wife. (Perhaps you could Google funny terms of endearment for spouses and find one you like.)

* **Something Funny About Where You are From:** This is a good place to find more than one thing and get a few more laughs. Make fun of being from the South, or a big city, or a farm town. One quick way to get to some laughs is to say, "You know you're from a small town when…." Google it if you need to. If there is nothing interesting about the city you are from, talk about the state, or the neighborhood, or even what kind of family you were born into. You know you're a military kid when. Brainstorm a bunch of answers and pick a couple of your favorites or ones that happen to be funny or interesting.

* **Share Something Interesting/Quirky that Most People Wouldn't Guess or is TOTALLY OBVIOUS about you:** Were you a Dodge Ball champ in third grade? Were you the picked-on kid? Do you have any freaky phobias? Finding out someone's odd little quirks immediately endears them to us.

* **Something funny about your job.** Many jobs are easy and fun to make fun. Think of the list concept. Ten signs you're an accountant. Google it.

Swanson Story-Libs™: The *You Need An Expert* Story-Lib

This is the perfect story lib to help you convince someone that they need your expertise.
This Story-Lib is intended to convince your listener that they need an expert.

Years ago, when I was _____ and _____.
How Old (Example: In My twenties)   *Give Us Context of Your Life at the Time*

something went wrong. _____ I figured that I
Name Something That Went Wrong That You Couldn't Fix On Your Own.

could save some money by fixing it myself. I had YouTube. What more could you need? Apparently,

you need more than a YouTube video. Sixteen hours, four hundred videos watched, three trips to the

store, and more money spent than I'm comfortable admitting – I was still no further than when I

started. In fact, my problems had gotten worse and I was in even deeper than when I started.

_____.
Make a joke about how your wife/partner/kids made fun of you

_____.
Describe some of the problems and the result in your life – money spent, energy wasted, etc

_____. I finally came to a couple of conclusions: Number one, I don't
Tell me how it made you feel

know what I don't know. I had no frame of reference. It was like trying to learn how to spell but you

don't know the alphabet. *(Or insert another example if you like.)* And, number two, my time is worth

money. And while I thought I was saving money, I was actually wasting money by using my time and energy and resources on something I knew nothing about. This was my first time trying to fix this, and I had jumped into the deep end of the pool without knowing how to swim. The expert has been working on this for twenty years. I get way more return on my investment by hiring the expert and focusing on what I do best. In two days *(or insert another time frame if you prefer)* everything was fixed and my life became

_____
Insert the result in your life of hiring the expert, beyond just getting the problem fixed – focus on quality of life.

_____. Lesson learned? _____. Why am I telling you this?
Tell me how it made you feel.   *Insert lesson—GET AN EXPERT*

Because many of the people I work with find themselves in this same position.

_____
Relate to how your customers try to do this on their own, state the negative results, and how it makes them feel.

They come to a place where they realize they just don't know what they don't know. I've spent my entire career studying _____. I've already worked through all
Describe their prolems and their pains in a short wayl

the case studies, and seen what works and what doesn't. When it comes to _____, we bring
state their problem

more than just solutions. We bring a team of experts who bring you peace of mind and make sure your money is working for you instead of against you. I would love to hear about your experience. Want to meet for coffee?

* Context of Your Life at The Time. For us to connect to the story, we need to be able to see it. Show us a little bit of you, the main character, at that time in your life. Tell us where you lived, where you worked, what kind of attitude you had (young and cocky, for example). What kind of dreams you had. We don't need a lot of details – just something to help us relate. For example: I remember when I was a young single mother, living in a cheap one-bedroom apartment, working in a grocery store, barely making enough to make rent each month.

* Something That Went Wrong. This is where you choose an analogy that your listener can easily relate to. Choose something that most of us can't easily fix on or own – computer, car, refrigerator.

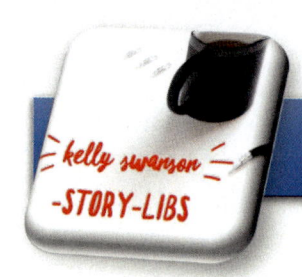

Swanson Story-Libs™ : The *Employee Appreciation* Story-Lib

This is the perfect story lib to help show employees how much they matter.
This Story-Lib is intended to **show your employee how much they are appreciated.**

The point of this story is to choose an example of someone you saw out there who really makes a difference for the customer and the brand of the company they serve. Someone who sort of mirrors the employees you are speaking to. Someone they can relate to being like themselves – or someone they can relate to having been impressed by.

There's this one place where I do a lot of business. _____. I'm in
Name the Store/Restaurant/Place of Business

there all the time. I spend a lot of money there. I've been going there for years. There many things I

love about the place - _____. But the reason I love
* *Name things that have to with the product, the atmosphere, etc*

the place is really because of one person. His *(or her)* name is _____.
Person's Name

_____. This guy/girl goes out of his way to make sure people have
* *Describe three things about this person* –

what they need. Even when it's not his job. He remembers everybody's name. He notices things about

them, like a new haircut, or a new car. He actually cares that you are there. He makes you feel special.

This guy who probably makes less than anybody in the place. I'm sure this company works really hard

to create a nice atmosphere, good marketing, and a quality product. But the real reason I keep going?

Is because of that guy. Why am I telling you this? _____. Because for every guy like this,
The Point of This Story

are hundreds of others just like him. The people who work behind the curtain. The people who take the time to notice their customers. These people are the ones that make companies great. Our customers don't do business with a building, or a fancy sign. They do business with people. At the end of the day, we are only as good as the people who tell the story of our brand. So today I just want to say thank you. To all of you who work behind the curtain – not just doing your job – but doing those little things that make all the difference. We are who we are, because of you. So when the days get long, and you don't feel like you make a difference – just remember this story, and know that you matter more than you may ever see.

* **Name Things About the Product/ Atmosphere:** You're about to tell a story where the lesson is about the people making the difference. So when you pick details about this place, don't talk about the people, but talk about the other things. For example: I go to this coffee shop downtown every week. I've been hanging out there for years. There are many things I love about it – they make awesome coffee, the chairs are super comfortable, and you get free WiFi.

* **Describe three things about this person:** Try to be a little creative. Pick something about their appearance. Something about their personality. Something about the way they act when they see you. Don't use boring canned words that don't really help us see that character – like "he was short."

Swanson Story-Libs™: The *Customer Testimonial* Story-Lib

This is the perfect story lib to showcase your brand through the eyes of the customers.
This Story-Lib is intended to share the story of a happy customer that you helped.

The key here is to pick a customer's story where their pain and emotion mirrors that of the person you are trying to persuade. You don't have to find customers who are exactly like this one, but rather customers who had similar experiences and even more important, similar emotions.

I'm hearing you say that you are struggling with _____ and
* Choose a Pain that Mirrors that of the Person Listening

that is making you feel _____ . This is not the first time I've heard that. I still remember a
Describe how they feel

couple /person just like you, who came to me several years ago.

_____. Their problem was _____ and it was making them feel
Describe him/her/them and their situation   *State the Problem*

_____. As a result, the impact it had on their life was that
Describe how they were feeling

_____. They had tried to get help before but it only
* Describe how their life was impacted as a result of this pain

made it worse because _____. When
* Wrong Choices They Made By Trying To Do It Alone, or Going to Your Competitor

they came to me, they felt like they didn't have any options left. And that's when we went to work. I

was able to show them _____. And how easy it was to fix it. Once we were
Solution You Have To Their Problems

able to _____ and _____, we noticed changes immediately! Within
Do What.   *Do What*

just _____ we saw amazing results. _____. The Impact on Their Life was
Amount of Time   *Describe Specific Results*

14

_____ and they felt _____.
Describe How Their Lives Were Improved in a Dramatic way   *Describe how they felt with this new life*

The point of this story is _____. It made me feel so good to know that I can use my
                              Point of The Story

knowledge and expertise to make a difference. They've been clients for years now. That's why I like

working here at _____. We don't just
                 Company Name

_____. We help people
Describe What You Do In a Boring Way Like Everybody Else Who Does What You do

_____. So let's talk about how we can help you
Describe it In a More Powerful Way that us Emotional and Personal

get the life you want.

* **Choose a Pain that Mirrors Your Listener:** Before you use a story to persuade, you need a very good idea of who you are trying to influence – their pain and desire and the emotions attached. If you don't know, then you need to ask more questions and listen more closely. You can often just assume their pain and emotion based on the customers who have come before them – almost as if you are using this story to help them identify the pain and emotion attached to their need.

* **Describe the Impact on Their Life:** A story becomes more interesting when we raise the stakes. So try to really show the emotional impact on their lives because of this struggle. Don't downplay it – overplay it.

* **What They did Wrong Before They Found You.** This is a chance to mirror the wrong choices that people make – especially when they go to others like you – your competitors.

Swanson Story-Libs™: The *Vendor Pitch Tease* Story-Lib

This is the perfect story lib to use at a conference or trade show as the vendor. **This Story-Lib is intended to tease them into coming to your booth for more information.**

This Story-Lib assumes that you only have a couple of minutes in front of your audience.

Hi my name is _____ but my _____ call me
      Your Name   *Husband/Wife/Friends/Kids/Neighbors*

_____ . I like
Insert Something Funny like "Guy who doesn't mow his lawn every week."

_____   _____
Something Normal You Would List on a Dating Profile'   *Something Else Normal You Would List in a Dating Profile'*

and _____ . My grandfather used
    Something Really Weird, Compulsive, or Silly About You – the More Absurd the Better

to always say _____. I learned that lesson the hard way when I was a teenager
              An Expression of Advice/Wisdom

and _____ . That was not a fun mistake to make.
    Tell Us About a Time You Learned a Similar Lesson the Hard Way

Today I work at _____ helping people to _____ so that they can
                Company   *List a Few of The Problems You Fix*

_____ and in turn, _____. I saw the lesson my
Describe the Results   *Describe the Positive Changes In Their Life*

grandfather taught me play out with one of our customers _____. They
                                                          Name Them and Give a Brief Description

were struggling with _____. They were feeling _____. We had a phone call
                     Name Their Problem   *Describe Their Emotions*

where I listened to their situation and was able to show them what they weren't seeing. They were

16

quickly able to see something they'd been missing. This one shift in perspective saved them countless hours, and a lot of money. I could see something they couldn't.

We help people see the mistakes that are costing them money, time, and energy. My grandfather also used to say that companies are only as good as the people who tell their story. We'd love to share our story and even more importantly, find out yours. We're in Booth 58. Please come by and tell us what you're struggling with and we'll share with you the BIGGEST mistake you might not realize you're making.

* Expression of Advice/Wisdom: The point here is that you choose advice that would fit your potential client. For example, "My grandfather used to say 'Price and Value are not the same thing.'   Google this to help you come up with something that applies to what you're selling. If you're a financial advisor, Google clichéd advice about money.

Swanson Story-Libs™ : The *PRESENTATION* Story-Lib

This is the perfect story lib to help you tell people what you do in an emotionally compelling way.
This Story-Lib is intended to **help you map out an entire persuasive presentation.**

Gathering Data: Just as with individual stories, the quality of your presentation and your ability to connect and influence, will depend on how well you know your audience. What makes them tick? What are their fears, their values, and the things they cherish? What are their struggles related and not related to your solution? How are you like them? What's your common ground? What are the feelings and emotions that you can relate to, and mirror in your own stories? What is their stated pain? What is the deeper pain? In my book, The Story Formula, there is a worksheet where you can process your buyer (listener) and find out some of this information, and then compare it to the worksheet you fill out on yourself, where you find the common links between you and them. **Connection is emotional and it is personal. People buy from people they LIKE, TRUST, BELIEVE, and FEEL LIKE THEY KNOW.** This template is designed to help you add connection and emotion to the information you want to share – and help you SHOW (not just tell) them how you can help them with their problems. A personal connection is what most people miss in their presentations.

***Who Am I** – This is the part where you (the "sales person") becomes a real person they can relate to.*

Hello. My name is _____ but people call me
                       Name

_____. I am from.
Nickame or Something Funny You're Family Calls You

_____. You obviously know that I am a
* Where you are from and Something Funny About Where you are From

_____. But a couple of things you may not know about me,
Job Description and What You Do

_____, _____, _____, and
Dumb TV Shows I Like To Watch   *What Pet(s) I have and their Names*   *My Favorite Music Group*

_____.
A Weird Hobby/Quirk I Have

18

In addition to all these things, I am a passionate believer in _____ so
                                                              Helping people to Do What

_____. This excites me because _____.
They can Have What   *List Why You Love The Work That You Do In Just a Sentence or Two*

Why Am I Here – State Your Intent Early in the Presentation.

In the time we have together today, I'm going to show you _____ ways to
                                                          How Many

_____ so that you can have _____ and get
Do What   *What Result in Their Life/Work*

_____. We are going to cover
Impact In Your Life on a Bigger Scale

_____.
Basic Things We're Going to Cover In Just a Sentence or Two

What Do We Have in Common and The Problem We Share – They don't believe you until they feel like

you "get them" and they can relate to you.

I know we have different jobs and different walks in life. But one thing we have in common is

_____ . and while I have a different job in a different industry,
State What You Have In Common On A Personal Level

I too struggle with ―――――――――――――――――――――― and because of this I feel
Big Overall Problem You Struggle With That's Similar to Theirs

_____.
Talk about how it feels to have this problem yourself

What Happens If We Don't Fix This Problem?

The thing is, if we don't address this problem, chances are it's only going to get worse.

―――――――――――――――――――― and it's only going to make us feel more ――――――― .
Describe the results and effects of doing nothing   *List Emotions*

Option: Tell a short story of someone who didn't follow your advice and the dramatic negative result in their life. Follow the story formula and don't forget the emotion.

What Happens If We Do?

20

If we do fix this problem, we can experience

_____.
Describe the Positive Results and Emotions

Option: Tell a short story of someone who did follow your advice and the dramatic positive result in their life. Follow the story formula and don't forget the emotion.

How I Experienced This Problem in My Own Life – or With My Customers

I struggled with this myself (or: I watched someone struggle with this) back in ―――――――. At the
                                                                                      Give me Time Frame

time, I was ―――――――――――――――― and I was struggling with
          Give Us Character and Context for This Story

_____. It made me/them feel
List the Conflict/Problem You/They were Having

_____.
Describe the Emotions

As a result ―――――――――――――.
　　　　　　Describe The Effects of This Problem

Shift in Perspective I Needed to Fix This Problem

Finally, I realized/learned that I was looking at this all wrong. I was focusing on the wrong thing. I was trying to ――――――――― when I should have been
　　　　　　* Do What

―――――――――――――――――. Once I was able to see my problem *(we were able to see*
Doing What

their problem) in a whole new light, everything changed. I was on my way *(we were on the way)* to

fixing it. As with most situations in life and in business, the answer is often found in the way you see it.

Looking at it from a different perspective can make all the difference. It's why most of the times we try

to do this, we fail. And we'll always fail.

So how do we make this happen?

Three Main Points that Helped Me/Us Fix This Problem

(Note: Audiences like things in compartments – understanding the order and structure of your presentation. Rather than give them a cobbled together collection of random points and advice, collect them into buckets. Most presentations have three distinct buckets. How much you say about each one is up to you. Just make sure it's clear what bucket you are in. Fight the need to give them so much information they can't process it all. Better to convince them they have a problem and show them a new perspective, and give some action steps – rather than tell them everything you know in 45 minutes. It's just too much. And if it doesn't convince them, or connect emotionally, you just gave a data dump. There's a difference in telling them what to do, and making them want to do it.)

(Note: If you have time, you can include a story with each point. Remember that a story is simply an example of your truth as it applies to real life. A simple illustration. If you have time, tell a short story. You don't need one under every point. You can even tell one story that makes all three of your points. A simple formula is tell the story, give the lesson, give them an action step – or simply ask, "So how does

this apply to you?" These stories are a great place to talk about the other clients you have worked with.

It gives your audience a chance to test drive your truth and experience the solutions you provide.)

Note: For now, you're just working on the back bone of the presentation. You can word it better, and craft better stories later.

Point 1 : _____

Story (Follow the Story Formula) + Lesson + Action Step

Point 2: _____

Story (Follow the Story Formula) + Lesson + Action Step

Point 3: _____

Story (Follow the Story Formula) + Lesson + Action Step

Note: How to handle the fact that you have more information than you have time:

An easy way to handle too much information, is just to let them know there is more information, and where they can find it. You can say something like, "I have six pieces to this system, but for today I am just going to focus on the first one. The others can be found in your handout."

I Know What You're Thinking (Obstacles We Ran Into)

(Note: This is the part of the presentation where you can address any perceived objections. The "Yes, Buts" tht you know the audience is thinking. Yes, but you don't realize how small our budget is. Yes, but you don't know the people I have to work with. Yes, but you don't know how much I travel and how hard it will be to follow your plan. When you can tell them what they're thinking, you will lessen their hesitation to follow your advice.)

As with most things in life, you will hit some speed bumps along the way. Things you will need to work out. I know what you're thinking. _____. These things
Name Three Things That You Think They Are Worried About

are normal, and we have worked out a system to help you through these obstacles. These resources are available to you: _____.
Name Resources – A Handout – More Info

The ReCap

Let's take one more chance to review the main points we covered today:

_____.
Recap BRIEFLY the points you made – the three buckets and shift in perspective

Action Steps

I've given you a lot to think about and process today. So let's give you some clear action steps you can take on Monday. This is what you should focus on first:

_____
Give them one or two action steps – and even have them share theirs with the group if you want.

Encouragement

I know it seems like you have a big mountain to climb. But once you start, you will find out that is easier than you think, and the results are going to be amazing.

_____
Give them encouragement to keep going – remind them how cool it will be when they start seeing amazing results.

* **Where You're From / Something Funny About It:** Make fun of where you are from, where you grew up, or what kind of family you were part of. Think of the list theory – ten signs you're from the south. Ten signs you grew up on a farm. Ten signs you are a military kid. Google it if you can't think of anything. No right or wrong answers – the goal is just to become human, create rapport and relatability.

* **What You Have In Common:** This is where you find common ground with them on a personal level and on a business level. Maybe you did their job at one time, or had a parent who did that job. Show them that you have some kind of personal relationship to what they do. Common Ground.

* **Talk About How This Feels to Have This Problem:** People don't relate to plot, they relate to emotions. When they recognize the emotion, they connect with their own story of a time they felt the same.

* **Character and Context of this Story:** Describe your main character. Whether it's you, or someone else like a past customer, tell us a little about them. Who they were. A few details about what they did for a living. A detail about what they looked like.

* **Shift in Perspective – Trying To Do What:** When giving a presentation it's often helpful to have one overarching theme. As the City Slickers guy said, "That One Thing. It's all about that ONE thing." You may have lots of solutions to fix lots of problems. But try to find one broad shift in perspective. Give them the idea that everybody is focusing on THAT, when they should be focusing on THIS. This is a good way to make it seem like all your competitors are focusing on the wrong thing and give yourself a leg up on the competition.

Congratulations! You now have the <u>foundation</u> for a compelling presentation. You still need to do the work to make it GREAT. But you a great structure, and a template you can follow over and over for each new presentation.

What takes this presentation from good to amazing? Humor. Amazing stories. Fun interactive activities. A story line that runs all the way through the speech. Just to name a few. And, yes, we can help with that.

Made in the USA
Middletown, DE
13 November 2023